How Things Move

Pushes

Sarah Shannon

Heinemann
LIBRARY

www.heinemannlibrary.co.uk
Visit our website to find out more information about Heinemann Library books.

To order:
☎ Phone 44 (0) 1865 888066
🖹 Send a fax to 44 (0) 1865 314091
🖥 Visit the Heinemann Bookshop at www.heinemannlibrary.co.uk to browse our catalogue and order online.

Heinemann Library is an imprint of Capstone Global Library Limited, a company incorporated in England and Wales having its registered office at 7 Pilgrim Street, London, EC4V 6LB – Registered company number: 6695582

Heinemann is a registered trademark of Pearson Education Limited, under licence to Capstone Global Library Limited

Text © Capstone Global Library Limited 2009
First published in hardback in 2009
The moral rights of the proprietor have been asserted.

Edited by Siân Smith, Rebecca Rissman, and Charlotte Guillain
Designed by Joanna Hinton-Malivoire
Picture research by Elizabeth Alexander
Production by Duncan Gilbert
Originated by Dot Gradations Ltd
Printed and bound in China by South China Printing Company Ltd

ISBN 978 0 431 19320 5 (hardback)
13 12 11 10 09
10 9 8 7 6 5 4 3 2 1

British Library Cataloguing in Publication Data
Shannon, Sarah
    Pushes. - (How things move)
    1. Energy transfer - Juvenile literature
    I. Title
    531.6'8

Acknowledgements
We would like to thank the following for permission to reproduce photographs: ©Alamy pp.**6** (Andre Seale), **8** (imagebroker); ©Capstone Global Library Ltd. pp.**10**, **14** (Tudor Photography 2004); ©Corbis pp.**16**, **23** (A. Inden/zefa), **5** (Gary Hershorn/Reuters), **21** (JGI/Blend Images), **19** (Laura Dwight), **7** (Randy Faris), **17** (Zave Smith); ©GAP Photos pp.**13**, **20** (Zara Napier); ©Getty Images p.**9** (Tony Anderson/UpperCut Images); ©Lonely Planet Images p.**12** (Martin Moos); ©Photolibrary pp.**18** (Blair Seitz), **15** (IZA Stock), **11** (Photononstop/Philippe Dannic); ©Shutterstock p.**4** (Maksim Shmeljov).

Cover photograph of a go-cart reproduced with permission of ©Getty Images (Stone/Peter Cade). Back cover photograph of a man pushing a cart reproduced with permission of ©Lonely Planet Images (Martin Moos).

Every effort has been made to contact copyright holders of material reproduced in this book. Any omissions will be rectified in subsequent printings if notice is given to the publishers.

Contents

Moving

Things move in many ways.

Things can move fast or slowly.

Pushes

You can push things to make
them move.

You can push things away from you.

You push a tyre to make it move.

You push a door to make it open.

You can push yourself up on
a see-saw.

You can push yourself along on
a scooter.

Heavy and light

Heavy things are hard to push.

A heavy wheelbarrow is hard to push.

Light things are easy to push.

A balloon is easy to push.

Big pushes

A big push can make heavy things move.

A big push can make things
move faster.

Stopping

You can stop things with a push.

You can stop a ball with a push.

Moving things with a push

A push can move lots of different things.

What things do you move with a push?

What have you learned?

- A push can make something move.

- A push can make something stop moving.

- A big push can move heavy things.

- A big push can make things move faster.

Picture glossary

push make something move away from you

Index

Notes for parents and teachers
Before reading
Explain to the children that one way of making things move is to push them. Demonstrate a few actions of pushing (e.g. pushing a door open, pushing a doll's pram, pushing a button on a toy). Ask the children if it is easy to push a heavy thing or a light thing? Show the children how you can move a toy car across the floor with one push.

After reading
• Give four children each a toy car. They should start from a starting point. They each have one push. Whose car goes the furthest?
• Stand the children in a circle facing inwards with their palms touching the palms of the children on either side. Choose one child to start to give a gentle push in one direction. Can they pass the push around the circle?
• Sit in a circle in the hall. Give each child a number. Give one child a bean bag. Call out a number and the child must push the bean bag across to that child. Then call out another number and that child pushes the bean bag on.